The Day I Lost My Wings

By

Antwan Deligar

First published in the United States of America.

Edited by Paul E. Jones, Ed.D.

Graphic Art and Illustration by Ahynte Designs

Published by I. M. A. Genius Publishing

A division of I. M. A. Genius Conglomerate, LLC

Printed in the United States

ISBN 9781733657808

Antwan is one of the most loving, compassionate, and family-oriented men I've had the pleasure to work with and get to know on a personal basis. He is the type of person who is extremely focused, puts his all into everything he does, and does his best to do right by everyone. Antwan is a person of high moral character and someone who will make you strive to better just by knowing him.

– Sergeant Major Marquis Woodland, U.S. Army

"Oftentimes the world seems like a very dark place... even with light it's hard to find your way... and then when you feel like the darkness will consume you... you reach one more time... hoping that you'll feel something... anything again... I reached into the darkness and Antwan grabbed my hand..."come on sis...I got you." When one thinks of a mentor, the likely person is always... this older distinguished person with a plethora of life and experience that you hope to one day emulate.... Not in this case... for many years I've looked to Antwan (many years my junior) for counsel. In my 20 years of military service... I've only found a select few that I would carry my burden to and that has been him... time and time again. I'm blessed... and I'm thankful for the light you provide and I only hope that one day my light will carry someone else through the darkness.
I love you Twan... you're the best little big brother a gal could ask for.

-Master Sergeant Ivy Krueger, U.S. Army

DEDICATION

To my wife and daughter, thank you for forcing me to become the man my father knew I would one day be. I love you, girls!

I dedicate this book to my father, Hezekiah Deligar III. No one has ever supported me the way you did. Your only requirement was that I hold my head high. I love you, pop!

Additionally, I dedicate this book to my Auntie Sariah Deligar. You always encouraged me to thrive in my creative side. I wish you were here to see this moment. I promise it's just the beginning.

Letter from the Author

Dear Reader,

Greetings! Thank you for taking the time to grab a copy of my first published body of work. I have to warn you ahead of time; this book is not religious in nature. I am a spiritual person, but this book speaks to moments of my life when I was very rough around the edges.

My paternal grandmother, Sarah Deligar, helped me realize that many people, some of which live in the very communities I grew up in, may not be privy to the medical treatment I was blessed to receive. Paraphrasing a little, she went on to say that my transparency could shed light on things some people might not be able to hear because they can't afford adequate medical care. I felt a responsibility to write this book and be as transparent as I possibly could. Please note that I am not a healthcare professional and cannot give medical advice. My comments are based on my experiences, treatment, and self-study.

I hope this book, birthed from my experience of continued recovery, plants a seed for people to not only get checked out annually but find positive ways to deal with negative things in life. Stress can be useful, but too much of anything can have a negative and possible long-lasting or permanent effect on your body.

Although I am on a spiritual journey at the moment, I felt it was important I stay true to my train of thought during the events I will discuss. Some of my language may be graphic, so I apologize in advance. This book is barbershop and kitchen table talk. It's a backyard BBQ discussion over a glass of cheap whiskey and a dark cigar.

I want to thank every family member, friend, leader, and mentor who encouraged me through my recovery and the process of writing this book. Most importantly, I want to thank Doctor Wheeler, Duke University Hospital Staff, Doc Vic and the entire Thor3 staff, my nurse case manager Sarah Dicks, the Fort Bragg Intrepid Spirit team, the Polytrauma Rehabilitation Center staff at James A. Haley Veterans Hospital in Tampa, Florida, and the USSOCOM Warrior Care Program (Care Coalition).

Although this book is a true story, I used pseudonyms for certain events to respect individuals and their families as it relates to confidentiality and privacy.

We look for perfection in things that were never created to be perfect.

MUFASA is dead!

Tearfully, I write this tribute to a person I wish was here to see this day come. He was my King, my Leader, my Protector, my Provider, my Disciplinarian, and though at times I did not appreciate it, he was the best example of a father he thought he was allowed to be.

Reflection

For most of my teenage years, I was upset with my father over things I felt he did wrong or could have handled better. In hindsight, I was an imperfect being expecting perfection out of one-half of the pair who made me imperfect.

Of course, I could list the discrepancies in parenting skills, but realizing he did the best with what he had, I must give him his due honor. Now that he is gone, the revelations have been immensely profound.

From adolescence to young adulthood, until we mature, most of us tend to shine a light on everything our parents have done wrong. In most cases, people learn a new perspective after becoming parents themselves. Many people let go and move on choosing to differentiate between what they will carry into their experience as parents and what they will not.

Others hold on to that bitterness and unforgiveness, waiting on an apology that may never come. Newsflash, the person who hurt you may not even know you are holding unforgiveness. Real talk, they may not even realize they beat you to a degree of resentment coming from you.

Consider this, we are selfish beings by nature. In many instances, we stop processing a situation after identifying our intent. We never truly consider the effect. Forgiveness is not for the offender. It's for you. Stop holding onto shit. You can forgive without putting yourself in the position to relive the experience. Accept the lesson, not the stressing.

Legacy

I am the only son of an only son's son. Confusing? Reread it, slowly. I think most sons want to make their father proud, but in the case of these sons, we all wanted to leave our mark on the legacy, which is the Deligar name. I never met my great-grandfather, but to raise a man such as my grandfather, he must have been pretty awesome.

In my father's eyes, my grandfather was the toughest Marine ever produced. When he spoke of his father, it sounded as if a young boy were admiring his favorite superhero. Based on the stories pop told me, in my eyes, my grandfather was a God-fearing lethal weapon. It took me a while to mature, but I eventually came to see my father in the same light, minus the fact he was in the Navy (friendly family rivalry).

No longer with us in the flesh, I reflect on the time I had with my father, and I think about the knowledge he shared with me from a young age. My father was not a street dude. He did not smoke, drink, or use a lot of profanity (at least not around my sister and me). My father gave respect to everyone, and he demanded it in return.

In my life, my father overshadowed most men in morale, posture, and demeanor. Many men thought my father was abrasive, but the ladies loved my father because he just had a way of making every woman feel as if she was the most important person in the room. Not in a playboy type of way, but more in the ultimate gentleman type of way.

My father gave me game on how to speak to people. Honestly, he would give it to anyone with the patience to listen. He always said to me, "I know you do not understand why I'm telling you this now, but you will never be able to say you did not know." The strange thing is, at that moment, I felt as if I was totally disregarding what followed that warning; However, there have been times when I could hear his voice, giving me clear guidance and remember where I was when he initially gave it to me.

Hezekiah Deligar III was my Mufasa! He was my king, who would let me wander into the elephant graveyard only to save me before my ultimate demise. My father is the reason I demand respect in every room I enter. He is the reason I give respect and feel that I should protect others. He was the reason I never neglected, nor will I ever neglect my responsibility as his only son and the continuator of his legacy.

My Mufasa is dead, but I see him in my reflection, and it is there where he speaks to me.

To my uncles: As tough as it is and will always be for you, I thank you (you know who you are) for being there by his side. I find comfort in knowing that he was not alone in his final moments. And to the uncle that busted his ass to make sure my father received the benefits he deserved as a veteran before he died, you gave him something that none of us could, a form of retribution. No matter how unappreciative others may be for the work you put in, I want you to know I saw it, and I know how much it meant to him.

Houston, We Have A Problem!

Is this how it ends?

"Sergeant Deligar, please move your arm so that the nurse can put in an IV."

------------------- A few seconds later ----------------------

"Sergeant Deligar, I need you to move your arm, please," said the doctor as her nurse began taking my blood pressure.

"I did doc," I responded.

"No, you didn't," she countered.

The look in her eyes sent me into a small panic.

"Sergeant Deligar, can you feel this," she said as she ran her pin down my arm.

"No, ma'am," I responded as I went into a full-blown panic.

Within seconds the skin on the right side of my face started to feel as though it was sliding off my face. My speech was becoming noticeably slurred. What I was hearing was not what I was telling my brain to say. The doctor and nurses were poking my right arm, leg, and foot, and I felt NOTHING. Full transparency, I thought I was dying.

Chapter I: AIRBORNE!

Do black people do this ish?

Never in a million years could you have convinced me, a guy from the Northside of Jacksonville, FL, would one day fly. Well, not actually fly, more like fall from the sky, putting my life in the hands of fate and my faith in a nylon blanket.

Up to the day I earned my wings, I did not think people of color jumped from perfectly good airplanes. At least not the sane ones. In fact, many of my family members, including my father, asked why I would want to jump from a perfectly good airplane.

For me, it was not for the thrill. It was for two reasons: to get out of my next assignment, and to get a change of pace. However, I was still curious and nervous at the same time.

I started researching becoming a paratrooper and learned about the 555th Parachute Infantry Battalion, commonly referred to as the Triple Nickels. When you get a chance, I recommend you Google search them. They are a part of black history within the military. Now, I was at least interested and challenged myself to overcome a personal hurdle.

I remember telling my friends I was submitting a packet to jump out of airplanes and hearing the almost offensive laugh that followed. It was no secret I had been afraid of heights my entire life. Hell, I still get a little light-headed on elevators and refuse to get on certain rides at the fair unless I have partaken of my liquid courage.

But after spending four and a half years in a Field Artillery Battalion, I came down on orders to go to Fort Sill, Oklahoma. I found out I was headed to an air defense artillery unit when a mentor of mine recommended going Airborne to change the direction of my career.

Mentor, Inspiration & Brother

Following my mentor's advice was the best decision I could have made for my future. At this point in my career, I had the pleasure of serving with some remarkable leaders, and some not so good ones. Unfortunately, there were more of the latter than the former.

I saw a lot of power-hungry selfish non-commissioned officers (NCOs) who acted as more of a mob than the backbone of the Army. I saw commissioned officers who were so political they sacrificed common sense for stroking each other's ego. I was tired of it all and concluded the military was not for me anymore. I was going to complete this contract and get out. The relationship I began to build with Lieutenant Colonel (LTC) Dwayne Dickens, changed all that.

When I first met Colonel D, as I called him, I was a junior enlisted Soldier (E4) stationed on Ledward Barracks in Schweinfurt, Germany. We both attended the protestant service at the local chapel on base. I'm not sure what led us to converse or even what the first conversation was about, but I remember thinking he was a cool dude.

To be honest, it wasn't until about our second or third conversation when I learned his military rank and position. I was a little intimidated because being in an artillery battalion and infantry brigade, junior enlisted soldiers avoided senior enlisted NCOs and officers like the plague.

I was shocked because he did not remind me of any other officer of his rank and position, I had encountered during my two and a half years of service. He was very relatable.

Eventually, we both joined and sang in the gospel choir at the chapel under my wife's direction. We weren't drinking buddies or anything, but I came to look forward to our weekly conversations. We spoke about Spirituality, Soldiering, and Mentorship. He was always pushing for me to drop a packet and become a commissioned officer.

I never saw a high-ranking leader appear to care about Soldiers the way Colonel D cared. I respected him so much that I asked him to come to my unit and promote me to sergeant (E5). He did not even hesitate to say, Yes!

I remember telling my unit I was having a Lieutenant Colonel come to the ceremony to speak on my behalf and promote me. Suddenly, my new battalion Commander, who was also a Lieutenant Colonel, was interested. He called me into his office to discuss who LTC Dickens was and how I knew him. I thought it was a little funny.

After my ceremony, Colonel D told me he was proud of me and told me my future in the military was bright. As expected, from our weekly conversations at church, he then threw in a shameless plug for me to convert to being a commissioned officer. He reminded me that the Army needed people such as me in the commissioned officer ranks.

Truthfully, until meeting him, I never considered becoming an officer. I knew they made more money, but I couldn't see myself getting far playing the political game that came with joining their ranks. Without even trying, Colonel D changed that perception.

One day at rehearsal, we were discussing being an officer. I told him I was not political enough, nor did I care to be. He said to me, "Antwan, this rank did not make me, my parents did. Changing the core of who you are because of what's on your chest is a choice."

For the first time during my short career, I started to envision myself becoming an officer in the Army. I began looking into the criteria for getting into the Green to Gold program. I met the educational requirement but needed to increase my GT score, which is a summarized score based on a standardized test of specific technical, mathematical, and comprehensive skills.

I promised Colonel D I would submit a green to gold packet. I truly intended to, but fear led me to procrastinate. I had a tattoo on my neck that led me to believe I had disqualified myself. He assured me it had not, but some of the white leaders in my unit made me feel otherwise.

I chose to focus on progressing on the enlisted side for now. I would accomplish something on this side and kept putting off submitting the packet. My excuse was that there was always one more thing I needed to do or achieve before switching over. I never did send that packet.

So, if you are reading this, Colonel D, I apologize for breaking that promise. I appreciate your continued mentorship, inspiring conversations, and brotherhood. Command Sergeant Major Steele, as a member of his command team, I appreciate you taking the time to help me take control of my career. Calling the Army Human Resources Center (HRC) on my behalf, even though I was not a Soldier within your unit, showed me that you genuinely believed every Soldier was your Soldier. I took your example and applied it to my leadership style moving forward.

Bengay and Heating Pads

I had just come back from doing a year-long deployment to East Paktika Province in Afghanistan. I made up my mind that nothing the Army could put me through could be worse than the things I saw and experienced over there. Although I was more nervous than I had ever been, I was ready for something new.

"Airborne school will be a breeze," they said.

Thanks to 12 months of seclusion from western civilization and a lot of iron therapy, I was literally in the best shape of my life up to that point. That being said, I still was not ready for the pain and aching I would have to endure teaching my body how to hit the ground. Bengay and heating pads became a nightly ritual.

Think of your best day crushing it in the gym. Remember how amazingly pumped you felt leaving the gym? Remember how horrible you felt the next morning? That is how my body felt every night of jump school. Every muscle in my body was sore, but it was fun.

Jump Day

I can still remember jump day at Fort Benning, Georgia. My very first jump, I was descending to the ground and could hear Sergeant Airborne yelling over the megaphone to slip left. This meant for me to gradually pull my left slip to turn my parachute in that direction. So, I did what he said and came in hot. I was 6 ft. 0 inches and over 200 lbs. Although the drop zone was softer than I had imagined, I hit HARD!

Sergeant Airborne came over to my landing spot and asked, "Damn Airborne, what was that?" I explained to him I was following his instructions, and he told me he was talking to the guy next to me. The crazy thing about the incident is the fact at least three other Soldiers were descending in the general area.

If I were an experienced jumper, I would have known to "HOLD WHATCHA GOT," as my Drill Sergeant would say. That meant I would have stayed the course and not made any adjustments. But this was my first jump, and my fear and nervousness led me to question everything.

While trying to get up to gather my parachute, I realized something was wrong with my left ankle. There was a sharp pain shooting up my leg that immediately caused me to sit down on the ground. I had to try to gather myself and my gear without bringing attention to my injury.

I could not let on to Sergeant Airborne that I was injured. We were told throughout the process any injury meant we would be recycled through the program and have to spend God knows how long on Fort Benning. That was not an option.

I was going to do whatever I could to graduate with my class. At this point, I knew more jumps had to be performed that day. Although I was determined to complete both jumps, I did not know how I was going to be able to do it.

I remember one of my classmates, a Marine Major, who motivated me to push through. This Major was an older gentleman. He was easily in his early 50's, but he was in the best shape I had ever seen anyone at his age.

He noticed I had a limp and came over to inquire what was going on. He knew if Sergeant Airborne caught on to my injury, they would pull me from the manifests and make me do the training over again.

17

The Soldier and the Marine

The limp was getting more noticeable, so Sergeant Airborne questioned my ability to continue. Trying my best to ensure I did not give off any signal of the amount of pain I was actually in, I let him know I was good to go. The Major helped me wrap my ankle tight enough to provide support and provided me with a couple of Ibuprofen 800 MG pills.

I am left-side dominant, so it was the side I felt most comfortable leaning to when doing my parachute landing fall (PLF). This is a sequence of events programmed into every parachutist to ensure a safe landing.

I figured I could just do a PLF using the right side of my body instead of my left. Since the drop zone was softer, it made continuing to jump feasible. The only difficulty came while walking on the injured ankle carrying my gear.

At one point, the Major and other members of my squad carried my gear, allowing me to redistribute my weight from my left ankle to the right and take some of the pressure off.

Long story short, with the help of my classmates, I made it through Jump Day and earned my Airborne wings. I was now a paratrooper in the United States Army.

As soon as I got back to Fort Bragg, North Carolina, I went to the emergency room. I had a severe sprain. I spent the next few weeks on crutches.

Just to clarify, I never really got over my fear of heights. Every time I got ready to board an aircraft, my stomach was in knots. I got motion sickness really bad, especially when the plane had to circle the drop

18

zone a few times for some reason or another. I would take non-drowsy medication for motion sickness before each airborne operation. But, the medicine did nothing for my nerves.

Before every jump, I would ask myself why the hell I was jumping out of planes. I had to tell myself it was worth the benefit of being close to home.

Mamma, We're Coming Home

With a little more than five years of service under my belt, I had spent the last four and a half years in Germany, and my momma made sure I knew she wanted me closer to home. Truth be told, even though my family and I moved a little over 300 miles north of my hometown, and she still felt I was too far away.

Marketta, my wife, was also from Jacksonville, so her side of the family was happy to have her and our daughter closer as well. At this point, I was not close to most of my wife's family. Outside of her baby sister, whom I had known since she was nine or ten, no one else approved of us being together or made me feel loved and accepted. In fact, at times, it felt like they went out of their way to let me know I should not be there. But if she was happy, that was all that mattered to me.

I knew that the next few years of my life would be a race to personal career goals I set for myself. With that in mind, I expected to do whatever the Army asked of me career-wise and wanted to make sure Marketta and Iyana were closer to their support system in the event I was on the road more than I was home.

19

Sacrificed Her Dreams for Mine

Looking in the rearview mirror, Marketta was always a rider. Simply put, she had my back when it came to my career. I appreciated that because moving to Germany put a pause on her dreams of becoming a nurse. Her choosing to move to Germany with me meant the world to me.

She didn't complain at all about the long hours or increased training and trips that took me away from the house. That actually made it easier for me to focus on the goals I had set and the actions I needed to take to achieve those goals. When I wanted to give up, she pushed me. When I wanted to explode, she defused me. When I told her my dreams, she said, "Why not?"

It was through loving and growing with her that I learned that imperfection in a traditional sense was more beautiful than flawlessness. Don't misunderstand me; the first half of our marriage was tough. Honestly, I didn't think we would make it to five years. In the back of my mind, I thought our move back to the states would result in us finally getting that divorce that loomed over our marriage for a while. Let me draw back the curtains a bit.

FROM THE MOMENT I SAW HER I KNEW I HAD TO HAVE HER...

FURTHER CONVERSATION REVEALED US AS KINDRED SPIRITS!

Chapter II: The Girl of My Dreams (Flashback)

Responsibility

Although I came from a family with dense military roots, joining the military was not my first choice. I was 19 when Marketta and I moved into an apartment together, and I officially took on the responsibility of providing for her and Iyana.

Iyana was not my biological child, but I loved her from the moment I knew she existed. In fact, when a scared Marketta came to me and told me she was pregnant and eventually admitted that the baby was not mine, I promised her that I would take care of them both if she kept the baby. Let me explain.

New Kid on the Block

Marketta and I met in August of 2003 at First Coast High School in our 12th-grade Physics class. I was a new transfer from another school and had come over to graduate with my older cousin, India. Her cousin, Meagan, was showing me around and introducing me to people. We entered our Physics class, and my attention was immediately drawn to the most beautiful creature I had ever seen.

She was 5' 11 with butterscotch skin, hazel eyes, and the shape of a grown woman. No, seriously, this girl was a brick house! Not only was she gorgeous, but she had a personality that matched her outer beauty. God's will was definitely working in my favor. Imagine how strange we both thought it was finding out, after class, that our lockers were right next to each other.

She had a long-time boyfriend that was attending Edward Waters College, the local HBCU. I understood that and was cool just being friends with her, but the more we got to know each other, the more we were drawn to each other. Long story short, she found out he had a girlfriend at the college, and our unofficial fling started.

Pregnant

Between late October and early November of that year, she told me that she was pregnant and that the baby was mine. I was a little skeptical, but I had fallen in love with this girl. I could see that she was scared. She spoke about possibly getting an abortion, and my response was, "Fuck No."

I promised her that if she kept the baby, I would take care of them both. I had just recently turned 17 in September, and she was now 18. We both had jobs at McDonald's and no real means of taking care of a baby. Still living with our parents, I told her that we needed to go sit down with my parents and tell them.

That was the scariest thing I ever had to tell my mother. My father was tough, but I knew his stance was that I would have to be a man.

Baby, Momma Drama

My stomach was in knots, but I didn't want my nervousness to make Marketta more afraid. So, I tried to play it as cool as possible. But I knew my mom was going to kick my ass right there in front of her. Although it didn't go that way, I could see the hurt in my mother's eyes.

My father asked me what I was going to do, and I said, take care of my baby. I told him that I would work more hours and try to get into the local community college instead of our plan for me to go off to college. Although I knew he wasn't happy, my dad looked at me with a look that only a father and son could understand.

My momma wasn't having it, though. Marketta took a pregnancy test right there, and the results confirmed that she was pregnant. But my mom kept saying, "Twan, that baby is not yours."

Momma's Baby, Daddy Maybe

I was angry with my mother because I felt she was just trying to prevent me from being with the person I loved and adored. At the time, I thought she was trying to protect her only son, but she ended up being correct.

I came to find out a year or so after we were married that Marketta purposely lied to me from the beginning, knowing the baby was not mine. A few months into our "friendship with benefits," I learned that Marketta was still involved with her boyfriend. I started dating a young lady, and Marketta thought I was going to walk out of her life forever if I knew that her boyfriend was the father.

Although we were officially and legally in a relationship, when I heard that news, it hurt me to my core. I knew Iyana was not my child before she was born, but I made a promise to be there for them, and I did. After I held her in that hospital room, sitting on the sofa, I knew I would never let her go.

I chose to stay local so that I could be there for her and Iyana if ever they needed me. I had to deal with the disappointment that my mother showed. I chose to give up the authentic college experience for a shot at proving I could be just as good of a father if not better than my own. There is more that goes into that, but I will not belabor you with the particulars.

I was in love with Marketta from the first day I met her and chose to be her fool long after foolery was suspected. This may sound crazy, but I felt terrible that she felt she had to lie to me. I knew she was the woman I wanted to spend the rest of my life with when we were in high school.

As I stated earlier, most of her family did not approve of the time we were spending together. As a matter of fact, while Marketta was pregnant with Iyana, her mom gave Iyana's biological father a car while her daughter was catching the bus come rain or sunshine with her granddaughter. For the life of me, I could not understand why this woman hated me so much.

One day while Marketta was at work, I went to sit with her mother to try and understand what her issue was with me. That yielded no fruit, but before I left, I told her that I was in love with her daughter and that I was going to marry her. I convinced myself that she nor her oldest daughter were in the position in life or relationship to tell me whether I was good enough for Marketta or not.

As soon as I established enough credit to get an apartment, I told Marketta we should get an apartment, and we did. I was the only one working for a while, but I had an excellent job out of town, and we were managing reasonably well. It was the three of us against the world.

No Love Lost

Marketta and I spent the next few years of our marriage riding a rollercoaster of pain, happiness, bomb sex, financial problems, more bomb sex, and trust issues. I was very immature and spent those years saying I loved her, believing I loved her, but not showing it. Operating in immaturity, I was purposely trying to reciprocate the pain and deceit I felt she dealt me.

On top of that, we had been trying, unsuccessfully, to have a child since the year Iyana was born. I am ashamed to admit; I was angry with her and God. I was mad with her because I thought she was secretly on birth control. I was angry with God because I felt I was being punished wrongfully. I was a hell of a provider for my family. Neither of them had to want for anything, but more of my time.

I started stepping out on my marriage and wasn't trying to hide it. I believed that my marriage was falling apart and that Marketta and I were better friends than we were a married couple. Every chance, I got I was throwing the hint that maybe we should consider divorce. I knew I loved Marketta, but I felt that we got married too soon and in our most immature state. Truthfully, even though we are in a great place, I still believe we got married too soon.

At this point, I was not bothered by losing my marriage. I was more exhausted from arguing over stupid shit with the only woman I could ever love in such a way. As Libras, we were both emotional and stubborn people. We did not like being wrong, and most of all, we did not like admitting it. We fluctuated between being the best of friends to not being able to stand each other. But when it came to the hustle, she had my back, and she knew I had hers.

Warning: Unsolicited Relationship Advice

A lot of women may not understand this next part, and that is fine. When a man is in a relationship with a woman, he considers being his best friend, continually arguing scares him. For any man worth his weight in gold, it should be a warning sign of a few things.

That being said, when a man is in a relationship with someone that they feel comfortable opening up to, they would instead break off the relationship than end up hating you or making you hate them. That may sound like an excuse, but the truth is a dish best served cold.

Most men will run in the opposite direction from that situation, thinking they are doing what is best. But it exposes how immature we can be, especially if you have a woman that is willing to fight for the relationship.

Notice I did not say fight for their marriage. See people that think they are fighting for their marriage are, more times than not, fighting against the shame of a failed marriage. It's not about the valued relationship. This is why you see people who have been married for a decade or two get divorced after the children are grown and out of the house. They no longer have to perform for the children and family members.

Cycles

Looking back at my 13 years of marriage, I was more afraid of staying married for the sake of Iyana. For a long time, that is precisely what I was doing. Eventually, my marriage became a routine from church on Sunday to our most intimate moments. It was evident that we were dealing with each other because we didn't want to become our parents.

Marketta's parents were divorced. Although my parents had been married all of my life, there was a time when I wished they had done the same. Some of the things my sister and I witnessed growing up, we should have never experienced, and if I'm keeping it a buck, I believe it affected how we viewed and valued interactions and relationships with people to include each other. But I digress.

I was in no state to give Marketta what she deserved. I will not go into Marketta's story because that is hers to tell, but she wasn't in a place mentally and emotionally where she could give me what I deserved either. Somehow, we had been riding this love with no helmet or protective gear and managing to walk away from mishaps with minor scrapes and bruises. But it's the invisible wounds that do the most damage. From infidelity and lies to poor money management, we had been through a lot.

As you have read in this chapter, we literally grew into adulthood together. Unfortunately, we never took the opportunity to figure out our own views on life and relationship prior jumping into a spiritual and legal union.

Throughout our marriage, I have received bad and wise counsel. To be perfectly honest, not many of those dudes survived their own marriages. However, the best thing I have ever done in my life was to visit a little church at the end of a dead-end road in Waikiki, Hawaii. The teachings I learned there were second to none. It's because of my time there that I truly started work on my relationship with Marketta.

**THE WAY A MAN SPENDS HIS SPARE TIME SAYS A
LOT ABOUT WHAT THAT MAN VALUES MOST**

SELF CARE & FAMILY MATTERS

Chapter III: Change of Pace

My Deer Friend

My family and I moved to North Carolina, and aside from being closer to home, I was also in a great unit. Now an enabler for Special Operations Forces (SOF), I felt as if this was a new Army. The late evenings sitting around waiting for the First Sergeant to release us, was rarely heard of. However, I quickly learned my new First Sergeant was a little strange, to say the least.

On my first day at the unit, everyone was preparing for what we call an organizational day. This was typically a day when everyone wore civilian clothes and had a chance to step away from the desk, even if only for a few hours. The day consisted of family, sports, music, activities, and food. I was no stranger to Org Days, but this one was interesting.

As I pulled up to the battalion building, for the first time, I saw a strange sight. There was a white gentleman with a deer hanging from the pull-up bars on the side of the building. From a distance, it looked like he was cutting it open. Curious as to what the hell was going on, I walked up to him. He introduced himself as First Sergeant Matthew Dumas.

Puzzled, I asked, "Ugh First Sergeant, what are you doing?"

He went on to tell me he stopped to grab some meat for the grill on his way into the office this morning. He was an avid bow hunter, so I could tell he was getting excited just talking about it. As he was getting excited, I was getting nervous. What in the world had I agreed to?

In all fairness, Matt was more level-headed than I initially thought and gave him credit for. When it came to leadership and the development of young troops, we had quite a few closed-door conversations that led me to gain a greater respect for him. As time moved on, Matt and I gained and continue to have a mutual respect that transcends our political and social views.

As I started recovering from my injuries, which I will discuss later in the book, we happened to run into each other again. He was a Sergeant Major now and dealing with challenges of his own. However, he still found a way to encourage me and has stayed in touch with me through this journey.

Matt, if you are reading this, please know your leadership was exactly what I needed as an introduction to SOF. As we have stated in private conversations, not many people understand us, but it's good to know we are not alone.

Time Value

Another big difference from my time in the conventional Army was the end of ridiculous and unnecessary formations. As long as I was competent and performed well, I had more time for my family and private education. Still focused on career advancement, I was not taking advantage of both.

I remember I was in the office around 1730hrs one day, and the Battalion Commander was walking through the work areas, saw me still sitting at my desk, and told me to go home. I explained to him that I found it easier to knock out my assignments before getting home because there were fewer distractions.

He said, "Staff Sergeant Deligar, you just need to find a way to balance it all. You must take advantage of the opportunity to have more time with your family." Reluctantly, I complied with his orders, but truthfully, I did not really understand at the time.

A year later, I realized exactly why the Commander was so adamant about maximizing family time. It seemed like I was away from home once every other month for some form of training or exercise.

My wife and daughter were used to me being away by now because I had two combat deployments within the four and a half years I spent in Germany before coming to this unit. Even when we were not conducting training exercises, it felt like we were at work forever due to poor task and time management by some of our leaders. Long story short, they deserved more time than I was giving them.

The Sacrifice

As I stated in a previous chapter, my wife was aware of my goals within this profession, so she never complained, at least not to me. That made it easier to stay focused on the grind. I knew if necessary, Marketta would find a way to intervene and let me know when it was time to take leave from work. In hindsight, I can now see that was her opportunity to max out her "honey-do list."

I freely admit I have a problem with being so focused on the end goal that I forgot to take a knee from time to time. If it was not unit scheduled block leave or for a medical reason, I rarely took time off from work. That was my first mistake.

Being a part of this type of unit allowed me to get military training that most people dream of achieving. With this in mind, I jumped at every opportunity to attend a school. The rest of my time went into college. I was determined to move up the ranks.

Tunnel Vision

I turned this opportunity into a side hustle. Every time I went on temporary duty (TDY), I made a little extra money. Those additional direct deposits became addictive. So much so, I started requesting to go on every TDY assignment or deployment I was afforded. These deployments were not as taxing as my previous two to Iraq and Afghanistan, but they were more profitable. Although I missed my girls a lot, I started telling myself the increased income was worth the sacrifice for now.

Here I was in a unit that afforded me more time to spend with my family, and I was nearly begging to get out the door to chase a check. Let's be honest, compared to what I could make in the civilian sector. I wasn't making much in base pay, especially since I had been promoted so fast in my career.

Dollar Signs

I was a go-getter when Marketta and I decided to make our relationship official, and she never asked me to change. That was one of the things I loved most about her. Marketta knew what I had been through in my adolescent years to young adult life and how I was motivated to create a better situation for our family. Admittedly, I was using the influx of income, which was noticeable enough to appease my family.

Another mistake I made when it came to my daughter was trying to substitute gifts for my time. Anything I thought Iyana wanted, I made sure she got it. I was tough on her about respecting adults, responsibility, and education, but the girl was spoiled since she was two years old.

ONE OF THE MOST DANGEROUS PLACES TO SOAK IS IN THE SILENT CORNERS OR YOUR MIND

LIFE HAPPENS! SURVIVAL MUST BE INTENTIONAL!

Chapter IV: Silence is so LOUD

There, but Not There

Even when I was home, I spent a lot of time in my bedroom or the man cave I established in our bonus room. So even when I was there, I wasn't there. Iyana would have functions and things going on, and I would stay home. One day Marketta looked me in my face and said, "Your daughter doesn't need gifts; she needs you."

The nerve of this woman to tell me in so many words I was not doing enough. Notice, she did not say that at all, but in my mind, she was ungrateful. My feelings about the whole thing made me seclude myself even more.

Although I had been with Marketta since I was 16 and she was 17, for some reason, after joining the military, we grew further apart. I felt like I wasn't the boy she fell in love with, and she wasn't the girl I could talk to about anything anymore. At the time, our marriage was a little more than two years old. Truth be told, we were losing it before it even started.

Bringing the War Home

Not long after coming home from my last deployment, my family and I were in crunch time to prepare for our transition to our next duty station. Between the mandatory unit reintegration, receiving and unpacking of equipment, and moving to a new duty station, I was too busy to really process what I experienced during the last year.

Marketta became concerned about the violent nightmares I was having. She pleaded with me to seek help, but I refused. Although the

36

military claimed there was not a stigma attached to visiting behavioral health, I saw otherwise. I heard the sly remarks by leaders and the rumors of ruining one's career.

Yes, First Sergeant

I lost my cool at work one day, and my First Sergeant pulled me to the side and said, "Staff Sergeant Deligar, you will go to counseling." How he said it led me to comply. Although my wife had pleaded with me to seek help, I felt that she could not understand what I was feeling. I knew that First Sergeant Jackson did.

I had always admired First Sergeant Jackson as a leader. He was overly competitive; he always had a clean-cut and was professional from a leadership standpoint. His stellar career was proof of this and became a model of mine. As a former Drill Sergeant, he was not to be played with or taken lightly. He was the type of leader that allowed you to grow as a leader. However, he would quickly call you on your bullshit and require you to do better. To this day, I still admire this guy.

Top, as we called him, didn't hover over or micromanage his leaders. As non-commissioned officers under his leadership, he expected us to do what the creed demanded of us, unapologetically. So, when he said, "go get help," I went.

Milk Man

Many of the memories that stick out from my last combat deployment to Afghanistan were so gruesome and feel so real that they have continued to haunt me daily. The smell of burning trash and dead flesh still takes me back to the middle of it all.

I remember one day sitting in my communications office doing an inventory with my Soldier and hearing over the radio that I needed to get to the tactical operation center (TOC) as soon as possible. When I got there, I was briefed that there was an explosion. Afghan troops were injured and that there were casualties.

We had practiced responding to such a situation as this, so it did not feel real just yet. Everyone quickly moved to their designated stations and prepared for the unknown.

Top said he wanted me to take two Soldiers and a gator (light utility vehicle) and head over to the gate that separated our compound from the Afghan compound to receive the injured troops. I could see the nervousness in their eyes and assured them that this is what we trained for. I told them to remember their training, take all instructions from the tower, and everything would be alright.

Although I had seen injuries and dead bodies before, nothing prepared me for what we were about to experience. I had never seen the human body mangled in such a way. I could close my eyes and smell death in the air.

I could hear the Afghan troops whaling as they stood by watching us pull their severely injured or deceased comrades from the transport vehicles. I remember opening the door to a Humvee and seeing what was left of a human body.

Seeing what war does firsthand was disgusting. Excuse my language, but that shit will forever be etched in my brain. Hell, the smell of trash burning flashes me back to some of my worst days on that forward operating base (FOB).

What the Hell Was That?

The worst memory I have is the day one of the Soldiers I was responsible for, took his own life. We were always ready because incoming rounds came almost daily. That day was different. I remember hearing what sounded like a gunshot. That was not uncommon, but the fact that it came from within the FOB was very troubling.

I remember running to the TOC to grab my M4 rifle. I carried an M9 pistol daily and stored my rifle in the TOC that day because I was going back and forth between the flight line and the TOC.

Some details of that day I cannot remember for the life of me. But I do remember hearing that the gunshot came from the Aide Station. As the headquarters platoon sergeant, I was afraid that one of our medics had a negligent discharge (ND).

That means that somehow, they mishandled their weapon, and a round was fired. Although we had not had one my entire time on FOB Boris, NDs were not uncommon, so much so that they usually carried serious punishment.

My heart was pounding because I knew Top would reprimand me if, in fact, an ND had occurred. Oh, how I wish it were a negligent discharge that day.

The Darkest Cloud Ever

The next thing I remember, the senior medic, on ground, came into the TOC to get help. I had known this guy since we were E4's, and I had never seen him this way. Usually, a comical guy, he was pale and looked as if he had been crying. I was not close enough to him to get the details of what was going on at first.

As whispers spread throughout the TOC, I overheard that one of the medics had shot himself and was deceased. The area was cordoned off while the DEA agent on the ground did his thing. It felt as if hours had passed before we were called to retrieve the body and put it on ice until a bird came to pick him up.

I walked over to the Aid Station with the First Sergeant, and the building was thick with emotions. As I walked down that dark hall to his room, which was on the right, it felt as if it was the longest walk ever.

When I entered his room, I could see his body on the floor, the rifle, the chair he was sitting in when he shot himself, and what looked like uncooked ground beef splattered on the wall directly in front of the door. I felt so sick I thought I was going to throw up, but I refused to let my superior see me crumble.

I knew that, as leaders, we needed to be strong not only for each other but for everyone else in the room. Emotions were high because this was a member of our team. This was a face we saw every day in the Aide station, dining facility, and MWR (recreation area for Soldiers and civilians on the FOB).

Once given the clearance, we assisted the DEA agent in putting the young Soldier in a body bag and taking him to the freezer.

The crazy thing about that freezer is that it was originally where we stored the food brought in by convoys from more massive bases. After that Afghani mass casualty, we used it to store bodies until their final flight would set them free from Boris.

What my First Sergeant did next made me respect him more than I already did, and I didn't think that was possible. He put the mental welfare of his troops first and proceeded to clean the room by himself. He knew that seeing our comrade's lifeless body would forever be ingrained in our memories. He wouldn't even allow me to help with the cleanup.

We had a few more incidents before we finally got out of that place, but we conquered every obstacle by facing them as one team.

SIDENOTE: DON'T LET ANYONE TELL YOU THAT ASKING FOR HELP IS WEAK. LIFE HAPPENS! SURVIVAL MUST BE INTENTIONAL!

The Afghan Sergeant Major

I remember the day I had to lie to a patient. The Afghan Army had gone out to conduct a patrol. The way the story goes, one of the Soldiers fell asleep on the crew-served weapon, and so the Commander started to smack him around. I know it sounds crazy, but there were a lot of things I did not understand about their culture. Anyway, the Soldier decided he had enough and turned his weapon on the Commander and Sergeant Major and fired.

We received the call that there were two injured and in critical condition. Although I was the communications sergeant, I was also the flight line NCO. I had a medical connex near my location that was used to treat patients until medevac birds arrived.

We were in the connex working on the Commander and the Sergeant Major. One of the docs and I were working on the Sergeant Major in the back of the connex while other personnel was operating on the Commander near the entrance. I remember putting the tourniquet on the Sergeant Major, while Doc put in an I.V.

"PZ-control, PZ-control, my Commander," the Sergeant Major cried. He always called me PZ-control, which was my initial call-sign while working on the flight line.

"Sergeant Major, I need you to calm down," I pleaded.

I could see that they were losing his Commander, but with his body facing away from the other stretcher that held his Commander, I had to give him hope. The last thing I needed was for him to panic. He had been shot multiple times. I did not know if he would make it, but at the moment, I had to tell him that he would.

"Sergeant Major, you are going to be alright. Ok?"

"Ok PZ-control, OK."

Knowing that he would panic if he saw his Commander's lifeless body, the other personnel removed him before we took the Sergeant Major to the bird. I remember that I kept telling him that he would be ok. But in the back of my mind, I felt that was going to be the last time I saw him alive.

He was successfully medevac'd, treated, and returned to the base a few months later.

When it came time for us to leave Fob Boris, I could not have been happier. I swore that I would never go back to that place. I swore that I would leave everything there and never look back. Unfortunately, that was not as easy as I had assumed.

Two Faces

I was able to mask my depression and emptiness with liquor and laughter. I started drinking heavily as a way to make myself numb to the things around me. I did not drink a lot in public, but if I had a gathering at the house or decided to have a few drinks alone, I usually mixed my liquor, making the effects greater.

Hiding my pain was not hard, because most of the people I had built relationships with were service members and did the same. From what I came to see, drinking was a part of military culture, especially for those returning from war.

At work, I was receiving recognition for my work ethic and commitment to the team, but I was drifting away from my family at home. I would come home, eat, watch television, and just live in my bedroom. In the darkness of my mind, the flashbacks were real, and the noise was loud. I hated being alone, but I hated being around people longer than I needed to be.

Drinking became a way of fellowship for those equally yoked in the battle scars, both physical and mental. The only time a red flag went up was when someone could not control his or her liquor and got violent, accident-prone, or tried to drive while intoxicated.

Throughout our marriage, the only time Marketta saw me drink heavily was after returning from deployments. I never did anything dangerous, but it was something she expressed from time to time.

One day she expressed her concern, and I never drank heavily around her again. If I did drink heavy, I stayed where I was until I sobered up. I never felt I had a drinking problem because I could go months and even years without taking a sip from a bottle.

All I knew was that alcohol seemed to work. I dealt with everything in stride resorting to a couple of shots of vodka a few times during the week to take the edge off. Sitting in a room expressing my feelings just felt weird. Honestly, I usually left angrier than I was when I arrived.

In my eyes, the second face I was able to maintain was working. As long as I stayed busy, I was productive. A few glasses of oil every night was not going to hurt me. In my opinion, it was better than taking pills that only required more pills to counter the effects of the other ones. You know, the expensive pharmaceutical addiction that we are given to suppress our fear of an untimely death.

Maj Jenson & CSM Jackson (humorously known as TMT),

I want to express my pleasure in having served under your command. The lessons I learned as a young NCO beside you in battle have forever shaped the human being I am today.

Quotes I will forever remember:

"Yeah, Buddy!"

&

"Hot chow, pick it up!"

IN THIS LIFE, PEOPLE WILL TAKE ADVANTAGE OF YOU. FAMILY WILL USE AND MANIPULATE YOU. PROFESSIONAL AND SPIRITUAL LEADERS WILL FAIL YOU BY ASKING OF YOU WHAT SOME AREN'T WILLING TO DO THEMSELVES. BUT WILL YOU ALLOW THAT TO STOP YOU FROM ACHIEVING GREATNESS? WILL YOU COWER WITH HURT FEELINGS OR EXCEL WITH FAITH AND DETERMINATION?

I REMEMBER RECEIVING THE BEST LESSON IN LIFE WHILE ATTENDING A TRAINING EVENT: PEOPLE CAN ONLY HAVE THE AMOUNT OF CONTROL OVER YOU THAT YOU ALLOW. TAKE YOUR EMOTIONS OUT OF THE MOMENT AND SURVIVE.

Chapter V: Promoted Myself Out of a Job?

*Disclaimer: This next section is my opinion based on my perception of the chain of events described at the time they occurred.

Promises Are Made to Be Broken

While on an assignment earlier that year, the Battalion Command Sergeant Major (CSM) had mentioned to my First Sergeant that the local non-commissioned officer (NCO) Academy was looking for NCO's so I submitted a packet to become an instructor, but I had to withdraw the packet once I made the promotion list. I promoted myself out of that opportunity.

Upon returning from that TDY assignment, I learned that we had a new CSM. His name was CSM Ryder, and he was a familiar face. He was a member of the battalion when I arrived in 2012. I also learned that the current non-commissioned officer in charge (NCOIC) of the battalion communications shop was retiring and that he suggested me to be next in line to take the position.

Although I had submitted my records for review to be selected for promotion to Sergeant First Class, I did not think much of it. I was sure a replacement would come before the results of the Sergeant First Class Promotion Board. However, upon returning, CSM Ryder kept saying that he wanted me to fill the position because of longevity and familiarity with the unit mission. He even made it a talking point with my First Sergeant very often.

Sergeant First Class (SFC) Joe Dirt

A few days before the list for personnel selected for promotion came out, the unit received a new NCOIC, SFC Mitchell. I wasn't upset or anything because I expected it, as I stated earlier. He seemed as if he was a good guy, so I conceded internally and just hoped to earn a position that would help me stay on track for the next grade.

Although there was one additional E-7 billet that was vacant, I was being told that I could not fill that position. That was total bullshit because I had seen it done before. SFC Mitchell gave me the textbook speech about why I should try to get on assignment to another challenging job for career progression. However, I wasn't buying that because I was fast-tracking and still hitting the essential career markers on my career path worksheet.

In all honesty, I had become so familiar with the mission, the unit, and what it took to be successful there that I was too comfortable to leave. This was the best unit I had been in, and I just wanted to contribute from a senior leader perspective. We had great Soldiers that I felt were not being used to their potential. Lately, we had been receiving leaders that were using the office as a transitioning point for retirement. Though those leaders deserved a slower pace in operational tempo, it appeared as if the Soldiers were suffering.

I knew that my branch officer would probably say I needed to leave Fort Bragg. However, due to my wife's job and my daughter's school, I did not see leaving North Carolina as an option.

Although I earned the right to succeed SFC Mitchell, every attempt to secure a follow-on position within the unit was now being shot down quickly. Although I knew I could stay there if I took my concerns higher, I could see that doing so would not be the best thing

48

for me to do. There was a new wave of egos and cowardly figures, and at the end of the day, it would affect the morale of the office in which I wanted to work. It was time to accept the inevitable and move on. I figured we would cross that bridge when we got to it.

Later that week, I had a scheduled airborne operation. I was always nervous about my jumps because of my fear of heights. Tonight, I just felt different.

That night I had a stroke, and my world turned upside down.

THERE IS NOTHING LIKE THAT FEELING YOU GET WHEN YOU ARE DRIFTING SLOWLY TO THE GROUND UNDER A PARACHUTE LOOKING OUT AT THE HORIZON.

THEN YOU REALIZE YOU ARE ABOUT TO HIT THE GROUND HARD AND MENTALLY GO, "OH, FUCK."

Chapter VI: Before the Stroke of Midnight

Just another Airborne Day

The day was November 8, 2016. I was scheduled to do a night jump with my unit on the Luzon drop zone at Fort Bragg, North Carolina. I was a little nervous for two reasons: I was jumping from a plane that I had only jumped once before; this time, I was exiting it at night. To be honest, as I mentioned earlier in the book, I was always nervous about jumping. What made this time different?

In hindsight, I can only conclude that the most significant difference that day was due to additional work-related stress. Specifically, the fact that I had just found out, I was selected for promotion to Sergeant First Class (E-7). I did not feel that the stress I was feeling was terrible. Honestly, I was just concerned and anxious at the same time about my next position. But that could wait. Right now, I just needed to make a good exit and a safe landing.

The Rush

After all, paratroopers loaded the bird, the primary jumpmaster (PJ) and alternate jumpmaster (AJ) gave the command, "Six minutes." Every paratrooper aboard the C-27 echoed the command. "Get ready," the jumpmasters barked. Again, we repeated the instructions to ensure every paratrooper was aware of our instructions at all times.

At this point, the bird is rolling down the runway, preparing to take off and drop another chalk (typically eight personnel for a plane this size). We rocked from side to side, front, and back as the bird went wheels up.

51

"Portside personnel stand up." We echoed the command. "Starboard side personnel stand up." We repeated the command. "Hook up." We echo the command. Things started to get real. Especially for a guy like me that hates even getting in elevators.

Most of us struggled to get to our feet as the bird is shifting, and our bodies follow suit. From here, the jumpmasters give the command to "hook up." I am hoping you get the idea by now that we echo every command. Here comes the most crucial part. The jumpmasters sound off its "Check equipment."

Both jumpmasters open the door located on their side of the airplane. They look out of the plane doors, hanging on to the door frame for dear life as they visually locate the start of the drop zone. They lean back in, look at each other, and give each other a thumbs up.

My nerves were all over the place as I prepared to exit the plane. Ritualistically, I start to ask myself what the heck am I doing jumping from an airplane. As always, I regain my composure, and almost exactly at the same time, I hear the jumpmasters yell, "Greenlight GO." Out the door, we started to go.

As I made eye contact with the safety, I handed him my static-line. Then, I executed a right face, squared up with the door, and vigorously pushed off and out the door, maintaining a tight body position. I couldn't have prayed for a better exit. "One, one-thousand, two, one-thousand, three, one-thousand, four- "as I had hoped, my chute opened, and then came the peaceful silence.

I quickly used the moonlight to help me orientate myself and the direction in which I was drifting. I noticed I was floating over the trees and immediately pulled down on my left toggle to get back on the drop zone. Then, I used my toggles to steer myself toward what appeared to

52

be a clear spot to land. As I got closer to the tree-line, I felt something was wrong.

Still, to this day, I can't explain exactly what I felt, but I just knew something was wrong. I made myself believe it was my nerves because I was concerned about landing in one of the many shrubs, trees, or holes in the drop zone. The fact that I had to blindly navigate away from all of those obstacles was even more stressful. But I was doing a pretty good job so far.

I have always been told not to look down when you are approaching the ground. Once you reach the tree-line, you are supposed to brace for impact. The reason they tell you not to do that is because you are more likely to tense up out of fear. That worked for me at Fort Benning while I was in Airborne School, but on Fort Bragg, there were just too many things that could go wrong. There were too many obstacles for any intelligent person not to look down.

I was so glad I was looking down on this night. If not, I would not have known that, although my brain got the sensation as though I had put my feet and knees together, my right leg did not move. My legs were wide apart, just dangling. Someone might ask, "Why didn't you just move your left legs over to the right one?" To be honest, at 248lbs, I was coming in so fast that by the time I realized something was seriously wrong, it was too late.

My life didn't flash before my eyes, but I did yell, "FUCK," anticipating that this was going to hurt. I hit the ground hard and felt my ankle snap. Then my head hit the drop zone HARD. It didn't knock me out, but it had rung my bell. I was dazed as if I had been punched in the head a few times.

I did not immediately feel the pain from my left ankle snapping. I looked at it, said a few more expletives and called my First Sergeant Richard Swartz to let him know that I could not move. I will explain why later, but my First Sergeant did not believe me initially.

The top part of my body was moving just fine, but I was in too much shock to move my legs. I looked down, and there was my boot leaning against my leg as though it had come off my foot. Then, I saw that my foot was still in the boot, and within seconds, the pain was the worst I had ever felt.

I threw my red chem light to let anyone nearby know that I was injured. I yelled for help, and a junior enlisted Soldier came running over. He looked at my ankle and used similar expletives to the ones that I had used. Then, I heard someone else coming. It was a Captain from my unit that I had seen around, but I never met him.

I could not remember his name, but I never forgot his face. I later came to learn his name to be Andrew Crowell. I remembered him because I remember he was gathering my parachute. Captain Crowell, wherever you are, you are a great American.

Before I knew it, a Humvee was pulling up, and I was being loaded onto the back. There were so many faces that I cannot remember all the names, and some of the faces are a blur. It's one person that I wish I could remember his name or even his face, but it's as if I have pieces of the picture at times.

I know you were a young Soldier because I feel as if I remember us talking as we were waiting to load the C-27. Although I probably would not be able to recognize you if I saw you, I will never forget what you did for me. I will always remember your poise in a very vital part of this story. Brother, I thank you for being the first on the scene. If, by chance, you are reading this book, look me up on Enterprise. I'm still supporting the SOF community.

Suck on This...

The guys loaded me onto the Humvee and drove me back to the rally point where a medical van was waiting to transport me to WOMACK hospital. As they load me into the duty van, I am still operating as if the only issue I had was a visibly broken ankle. I had convinced myself that I had made a rookie mistake, and my broken ankle was the price I had to pay. The pain was excruciating. The senior medic on ground hands me a lollipop and tells me to suck on that. I thought he was trying to be comical and asked him what the hell was this? He was trying to explain that it was a medicated lollipop, but I was used to the guys making jokes, especially about rookie mistakes, so I wasn't trying to hear it.

My First Sergeant and one of the other medics on the scene was like, "no, seriously, it is medicated." I did as they said, and it definitely took some of the pain away.

They rushed me to the hospital, and I was taken to the back to be treated. At this time, I am still being treated as a patient injured on a jump resulting in a broken ankle. I don't remember when I called Marketta, but she was there within, what felt like minutes, of me being there. Note that we lived 25 minutes away from where I was at the time.

The nurses started to treat me as I watched the results of the election slowly come in on the television in my room. It was official that Donald Trump was our new president and my new Commander in

chief. It was a little funny because one of the nurses started crying.
Marketta and I looked at each other humorously because she was
seriously upset that her choice did not win. She was a sweetheart,
though.

As the nurse worked on me, I was thinking about how I had made
a rookie mistake, and now my ankle was broken. I was still not sure
why my brain was being told my feet and knees were together, but my
feet were not coming together. As a staff sergeant, I was embarrassed
and confused at the same time. One of the medics from my unit stayed
with me the whole time until my First Sergeant arrived. Thank you,
Higgy, for being there by my bedside. Brother, I will never forget that.

Richard "P-Nut" Swartz

Speaking of my First Sergeant, I was convinced that knowing Rich
was going to kill me. Earlier that year, he took me on a hike in Hawaii.
No BS, the damn trail up the mountain was missing a few stairs here
and there the higher up we got. Oh, and it was raining that day. I'm
sure I don't have to tell you what happens when wood gets wet.

Then, we went kayaking a few weekends later, and he almost
drowned me by flipping the kayak over in rough waters chasing after
his phone. Once I calmed down, I stood on something that felt as if it
was a rock, caught my breath and got back in the kayak. He thought it
was the funniest thing in the world. I was pissed. But like always, we
had a drink, and we were on to the next adventure.

As much as I hated Rich's adventures, I loved the fact that I had a
friendship that pushed the limits of my comfort zone. If it weren't for

our mutual friend Ivy, Rich and I would probably have done more insane stuff.

I thought the madness ended in Hawaii, but shortly after everyone returned from our planned vacation, he was back on that bullshit. Ole P-Nut tells us that we are doing an eight-mile ruck march, and that was no problem. The entertainment came when we got eight miles into the movement and had not reached the turnaround point yet. Oh, and we did it on the hottest day EVER. This guy was out of control.

I ended up going to the Emergency Room because I lost peripheral vision in my left eye, and it felt as if someone drove a needle through my right eye. They diagnosed it as a migraine, gave me medicine intravenously, and within a couple of hours, I was discharged from the hospital. I blame Rich for the whole thing.

Things Got Weird

Getting back to the story, the doctor came in to evaluate me while the nurse was taking my vitals. The last thing I felt was the blood cuff squeeze on my arm. I started talking to Marketta to assure her I was going to be ok.

"Sergeant Deligar, please move your arm so that the nurse can put in an IV."

I did as she asked.

------------------ A few seconds later ---------------------

"Sergeant Deligar, I need you to move your arm, please."

57

"I did doc."

"No, you didn't."

The look in her eyes sent me into a small panic.

"Sergeant Deligar, can you feel this?"

"No, ma'am."

At that moment, everyone kicked into gear and realized something else was wrong. My speech instantly started to slur, and the doctor asked me to look at her. As I followed her instruction, I began to think, what in the world is going on?

My brain was getting the sensation as if my arm was moving, but when I looked over at my right arm, it did not budge at all. Seconds later, the right side of my face started to feel as though the skin was falling off of it. At that very moment, I began to freak out. Truthfully, I thought I was dying.

And just that F.A.S.T, I was having a full-blown stroke. That team of medical professionals was terrific. They responded to the situation quickly and, in turn, saved my life.

They gave me a shot that would reverse the effects of the stroke. Four and a half hours went by, and it seemed as if they did every test in the world. You guys must understand that the quick response to the stroke symptoms is what saved my life as I know it. Although this may be an exaggeration, it seemed like every 10-15 minutes, I was going somewhere to have a test done, or someone was bothering me. I was in my emotions and just wanted to be left alone.

The Life That Flashed Before My Eyes

Tears rolled down my face because I could only think about the things I would never get to do with my daughter. Things such as taking her hunting, riding ATVs, watching her graduate high school and college, and walking her down the aisle on her wedding day. My emotions were all over the place. I thought I was going to die, but I wasn't afraid of death in and of itself. I was worried about leaving my daughter without a father. As I think back to that day, it wasn't my life that flashed before my eyes. It was hers.

I remember praying to God for more time to get it right. I wasn't praying out of fear of going to hell. Instead, I was praying for more time to fix the many missed opportunities to spend valuable time with Iyana. She meant the world to me. Every day of my military career and deployment that came with, it was worth the headaches because I was able to give her a life I didn't have.

My biggest mistake, however, was not giving her a lot of my time. I let mental and physical exhaustion become my excuse to come home and stay in my room. I substituted giving gifts for my time, and that was not fair to her. Dear God, what had I done? I had gotten caught up in being a provider that I lost the importance of being a dad.

Miracle on 2817 Reilly Road

Before I knew it, hours had passed, and I was still paralyzed on my right side. My face was still drooped, and my speech was slurred. The male nurse was poking the bottom of my feet with some type of object, but I couldn't feel anything. He left, and I remember telling my leg to move, and it did. Doc Wheeler came in, and I said, "Doc, I can move

59

my leg." She said, "No, Sergeant Deligar, you cannot." I proclaimed to her that I could and proceed to move my leg, and she immediately said, "Oh my God." She yelled for the nurse, and within seconds, I could feel my face returning to normal. My wife witnessed the whole thing.

At this moment, the room was thick with emotions as everyone in the room was either in tears or visibly in shock and disbelief. The doctor was in tears, and she hugged me. I will never forget that because I had seen my fair share of trauma, but never had I seen God receive all the glory in a military hospital. As my spiritual father would say, "Please don't hear what I am not saying." I know that many people are working in the medical field that follow the Christian faith, but the emotions in that room were like nothing that I had experienced before.

While all of this was occurring, the doctor had already been working on sending me to the University of North Carolina (UNC) hospital. She told Marketta and me that there were limited resources in the base hospital and that she felt we needed to get there. She warned us that the most significant issue would be getting a bed. She also reached out to the staff at Duke. Now we just had to play the waiting game. And wait we did.

It took a few hours, but we somehow managed to get a bed at Duke. I was medevac'd to Duke by helicopter, which was FREAKING AWESOME, by the way! When I arrived there, it felt as if all hands were on deck. If you remember, I snapped my left ankle due to the partial paralysis and the inability to control my lower body. My left knee, left hip, lower back, and neck was in pain too, but they had to focus on the most emergent issue.

They put an air cast on my left leg and treated my stroke symptoms over the next few days. It was actually kind of cool because hot nurses and college girls were coming in checking on me daily. Marketta was said, "Oh, your speech gets better when they come in, huh?"

Dad, I'm Ok...

I remember my pops coming up from Florida with my mom and baby sister. He was not okay with what he saw. He kept it together in front of my mother, but when the girls left to grab some things from the store, I could see that he was concerned. At one point, he was about to regulate because he felt no one was moving fast enough for him. Although my speech was badly broken, I told him it was fine. At that moment, I could see that he felt he was protecting his little boy and not his grown son. It warmed my heart a little.

Ivy and Rich,

I appreciate you guys being genuine. Rich, your friendship comes with life risks, but I wouldn't trade that shit for another one. Ivy, I love you. You are the most kindhearted person I know. I couldn't have chosen a better godparent for my child. I value your unwavering friendship.

Thank you both for being there at the scariest part of my life. Our humor could make the toughest moment not seem so bad.

62

YOUR VALUE IS YOURS TO DETERMINE!

**PLACE IT IN THE HANDS OF ANOTHER, AND YOU
WILL DECREASE AS THEY SEE FIT!**

Chapter VII: No Time to Heal

One Medical Crisis after Another

I had my stroke on November 8, 2016. On November 19, 2016, I had to have surgery to repair the damage done to my left leg during the airborne operation. After having a stroke, I found out that I had an atrial septal defect (ASD). Less than a week later, I had a pulmonary embolism. To add to my misery, I was placed on blood thinners and now having small seizures.

The Atrial Septal Defect

While I was being evaluated for damage caused by the stroke, the doctors found a hole in my heart. The military doctors said it was something I was born with, but this was news to my parents and me. My pediatrician never mentioned such a diagnosis. The rigorous physicals I endured after suffering an incident in basic training, nor the examinations I went through before my combat deployments gave any indication that there was a hole in my heart.

My wife and I were perplexed but had no time to dwell on the shock. The cardiologist and neurologists at Duke believed that my vigorous thrust from the C-27 platform caused a blood clot to travel up my leg and pass through the ASD toward the left side of my brain. That clot is what led to me having an ischemic stroke. An ischemic stroke occurs when blood cannot reach the brain. According to Google, a blood clot blocks the vessel that carries blood to the brain.

Pulmonary Embolism

A few days before Thanksgiving, I was having what felt like tightness in my back from the base of my neck to the lower part of my trapezius. I took a few muscle relaxers and chalked it up to my body, adjusting to the previous events it had just experienced.

On November 23, 2016, the pain had become so bad that it woke me from my sleep. I told Marketta that this wasn't just tight muscles. My chest was hurting like never before. She called the nurse on call with Tri-Care, and they told her to have chew baby aspirin and call an ambulance immediately after hanging up with her.

I told Marketta that I needed her to call my father. I knew if anyone could talk me through this pain, it was him. Not only was he the strongest man I knew, but he was also a survivor of multiple heart attacks. I was scared, but he calmed me down and told me everything would be alright. He was right. It turned out that I did not have a heart attack, but I did have a blood clot in my lungs, and that was serious.

I Think I Need Rehab...

In a matter of 30 days, I had suffered a small stroke, full-blown stroke, a concussion, broken bones, been paralyzed, had surgery to repair the broken bones, and experienced a blood clot in my lungs. Those chain of events led to me being out of work for 45 days. During that time, my wife busted her ass to make sure that I was getting some kind of therapy.

Her mom even came to Fayetteville, NC, from Jacksonville, FL, to take care of me while Marketta headed back to work. That was a significant sacrifice for her at the time, and it meant a lot to us that she cared enough to come to give her a much-needed break. In Marketta's eyes, though, nothing the military was doing was happening fast enough. Eventually, I was able to get into physical therapy at Thor3, with Doctor Victoria Rath, and receive rehab for a much of my cognitive issues at the Intrepid Spirit on base. The entire team at both centers were terrific.

Doc Vic started working with me on speech before I was able to get into speech therapy. She would make me recite certain things while doing my required physical training. It was easy to see that she loved what did for a living and was dedicated to not just getting me back in the fight, but ensuring that I was truly healthy.

My time at the Intrepid Spirit was a significant part of the rehabilitation process. The staff was tasked with helping me repair my cognitive skills, vision, and speech. Aside from the damage, my body had suffered, I was also dealing with issues related to my speech. I never stuttered in my life, but since my stroke, I struggled to find word placement quite often. Anxiety and exhaustion made it worst.

The staff at the Intrepid Spirit recognized that I could get better help at a polytrauma rehabilitation center. The nurse case manager was able to get me into the program, and within a few weeks, I was flying into Tampa, Florida.

When I arrived at James A. Haley Veteran's Hospital, I was received in the Polytrauma ward and got a chance to meet some pretty awesome people. From the nursing staff to the doctors and therapists, to my fellow program participants, the experience was what I needed. I was fortunate to be a part of such a program.

At one point, I even got to record an original song in a real studio thanks to the Guitars for Heroes program. They also allowed me to bring my buddies from the program to share the experience.

If It Ain't Broke...

Long story short, I was broke as fuck, meaning I was a medical mess. Although the medical team was accommodating for most of my issues, my rehabilitation process was not one hundred percent successful. I spent most of the time frustrated because I was not allowed to push myself in physical therapy due to the hole in my heart.

I was not allowed to get my heart rate over 130 bpm, and though this might be a slight exaggeration that felt like a slow crawl for me. I was given a watch to monitor my heart rate and had no wiggle room on the max rate. I was miserable sitting in the physical fitness sessions.

In hindsight, I complained a lot because I felt they should not have accepted me into the program if they were not going to allow me to get the most out of the program experience. I wished they would have required the hole in my heart to be fixed before coming into the program. Nevertheless, the other people in the program with me encouraged me, and we got through it together.

To my fellow PREP team members: I won't say your names out of respect for your privacy and lines of work, but I appreciate each of you. I remember telling you guys one day that I would write this book, and here it is two years later.

While I was in the PREP program, I was able to get Duke to schedule my ASD closure. I opted to leave the program a little early to get back to North Carolina, so I could get the hole in my heart closed. It was the only way I would ever be able to do any real physical rehabilitation.

At times, I felt the doctors and therapists didn't understand my frustration, but I hope this unfiltered look into my train of thought will help. I was a part of the Special Operations community. Although I was an enabler, I spent most of my time in the military trying to prove to the infantrymen and operators that using my brain for a living didn't make me weaker than them.

You're Just the Commo Guy

Just to explain a little, an enabler in the military is a person that provides a skill that enables the operator to focus solely on his or her job. These skills can include human resources, logistics, communications, medical support, etc. I was a communications specialist, and I loved my job.

After joining the SOF community, I realized very quickly that you had to have at least three attributes to thrive. In essence, you must be physically fit, know your job, and not take shit from egotistical personnel that rarely knew their jobs. I refused to just be the commo guy.

Whenever I deployed in support of my company, I made sure that I learned how to do more than just set up their communications. I helped run the operations center, advised joint signal personnel from time to time, and even took over as the SARC for the entire task force in the Philippines under Colonel Eric Brown. All in all, I just wanted to be a part of the team and for my guys to know they could trust me.

Don't misunderstand me, I wasn't a door kicker, but I wasn't a bullshitter either. I had to make sure I was an asset to the command and not a lazy liability. That led to the opportunity to work with every entity of the Special Operation community except the Pararescuemen (also known as PJs).

At one point, I even caught the bug and considered taking a shot at becoming an operator. Then, I realized that there weren't many people that looked like me that appeared to feel comfortable in their skin once they crossed over. Don't get me wrong, there were a few solid people of color on the other side, but there weren't many.

From choosing to overlook blatant racism from their peers to failing in mentorship and development of the young people of color hoping to follow in their footsteps, the ball was repeatedly dropped. At times, it felt like the Wild West, and every man and woman was for themselves. Therefore, I chose to stay in the communications field. That was the best decision I made in my latter career.

To My Mother-in-Law (Mom),

Filled with emotion, I write this thank you letter out of appreciation for what you did for us. In December of 2016, you took off from your job, risking losing your source of income to drive to Fayetteville and stay with us so that you could take care of me, while Ketta went back to work. I will never forget that you fed me, helped me get around, and just gave Ketta the rest she needed. For the first time since marrying your daughter, I felt as though I was your son. I am forever grateful for the sacrifice you made for us.

Contrary to our expectations, family won't be perfect. It's the process of growth and maturity. I am blessed to call you family.

Chapter VIII: This Is the End

Wasn't Healing Fast Enough

Thanks to a buddy I met while attending a victim's advocate training in Florida, less than a year prior, I was able to get that position that I told you I wanted earlier. He introduced me to his Command Sergeant Major, CSM Swagg, and the rest was history.

I hit the ground running and did my best to improve the work environment daily. Sometimes that being tough as nails, having compassion for other's situations, and being that mentor and example that I saw less and less of in this new selfish culture. I didn't always get it right, but dammit it wasn't because I chose not to try.

After I had the Pulmonary Embolism, my doctors started suggesting that I consider a medical separation from the Army. They were concerned about the multiple life-threatening events that I had encountered in such a short time. I didn't even entertain it. I had found something that I was good at and could see continuing growth. I wasn't ready. So, I pressed on and did what I had to do.

My goal was to leave a professional impression on the lives of young Soldiers and my fellow leaders. Due to the relaxed nature of our environment, some Soldiers and leaders alike thought that meant being friends. However, many didn't know how to balance personal and professional expectations, and I refused to put myself in that position. Honestly, I was very paranoid about relationships in the workplace. I had leaders that I respected as mentors and later as big brothers and sisters, but I didn't trust most of my peers or subordinates.

Remember First Sergeant Jackson, from my Afghanistan deployment? When I became a non-commissioned officer, he was my first mentor, and he would always say, "Deligar, Joe will fuck you every time. You must lead them, not be their friend." He was right, as usual.

Looking in the rearview mirror, I wish I knew then the internal peace I know now. I probably would have fussed and cussed less and improved my leadership style while attempting to adapt to each person. To the leaders reading this book, that doesn't mean giving in or being weak.

I am proud of what we were able to accomplish as a team in my communications shop. But what I am alluding to is that as I matured, I recognize that different people are motivated and inspired by different things. Honestly, it's as if you are raising children. What works for one of your children may not work for the other child. So your style of parenting or leadership, as it pertains to Soldiers, must be adaptive.

Ticker Still Ticking.

Within my first few months in a new unit, I had heart surgery and then knee surgery 30 days later. A month or so after that knee surgery, I was helping a Soldier move some office equipment and was shocked by electricity and burned my hand pretty bad. That Soldier later joked that he thought I was dead when he saw all those sparks flying. Of course, he ran… jackass!

He took me to the Emergency Room, and when the doctor saw my recent history, she joked that I might be missing the hints. I think she was onto something. It did feel as if I was playing Russian roulette with death, but hell, I was winning. "Just make sure my ticker is still ticking and get me out of here." That's all I was thinking. I was tired of hospitals at that time. They kept me overnight for observation because of the recent heart surgery and released me back to duty.

The Stress Was Killing Me…

Due to rapid changes and a high operational tempo, things quickly got busier than I expected. At first, my biggest hurdle was changing the culture of our office and getting my troops to produce quality work in a timely manner. Remember, I told you this environment was a little more relaxed than other conventional Army units. Unfortunately, the troops were taking advantage of that in the wrong way.

I had great troops, but they were not working or leading at the level I knew they should be. In fact, most of the shop depended on one Soldier, junior in rank, to fix many of the issues or give direction. That disgusted me, and I made it known. That was too much pressure to put on that Soldier and not enough responsibility spread across one of the largest shops in the battalion.

The necessary change was tough to implement. I had fellow leaders from other offices undermining me to the troops. I had a bit of insubordination within my shop that even went as far as to get me placed under investigation based on lies. The Soldier said that I would come to work high off of drugs and create a hostile environment. The only pills that I took were prescribed, and when I noticed one of them made me a little sluggish, I immediately asked the doctors to change it. It was unfortunate that she would use my uncontrollable situation to try and save face because she was being exposed as a liar and fraud on so many levels.

I took the drug addict part personal, and it made me feel defeated for a while because Soldiers were my life. I would never put them or their safety in jeopardy. I had never had someone lie on me in such a way, but it was later revealed that that person had a history of filing reports when she didn't get her way. She was used to batting her eyes to get out of trouble, and I was determined to force her to lead at the level the Army promoted her to or higher.

As a former advocate for victims, I took this process seriously because I realized that many investigations result in favor of the most popular and not the innocent. I was the new kid on the block and got pretty good at ruffling feathers, as I attempted to change the culture around me, so I had no one to fight for me except my supervisor

(Thanks, Octavia). Fortunately, the investigation went in my favor, and I was able to continue leading our shop in the right direction.

Soldiers were getting promoted the right way, and their efforts were being recognized across the battalion. In the end, it was worth it to see many of them move on to do great things. I don't want the credit for that. I do want each Soldier that I have led to know that you are where you are because you made a conscious decision to change the direction you were heading. Remember that because one day, you may have to be the one implementing change somewhere.

Family Life Was Declining Again

Things at home were awkward at best. I started detaching myself from Marketta and Iyana mentally and emotionally. I didn't like how I felt about myself, and I was feeling like they were watching me decline. I'm sure they both felt like I was falling into the deep mental foxholes I dug for myself after my return from Afghanistan. But I was actually tired of feeling like a patient to the sexiest woman I knew. Even though she never made me feel like less of a man, my pride told me otherwise.

When my speech would slow down nightly, the look in my daughter's eyes made me feel like I was scaring her. The worry in her eyes was clear and there was nothing I could do to control it. I separated myself from them whenever I was home and actually found more reasons not to be home. From an increase in official travel to just hanging out more, I was in the process of throwing my family away and I didn't realize it.

My medical treatments were ramping up and so were the effects of the medicine. I hated life. I was self-destructing and the people around me were helplessly watching and sometimes became victims of my mood swings and brokenness. I appreciate you all for your prayers, encouragement and most of all for not giving up on me.

Time to Hang It Up

Eventually, I noticed my speech was getting slower at work and keeping up was becoming more of a task. Most of the time, I was able to conceal it at work. However, when I got home, I couldn't hide it from my wife and daughter. My speech would slur dramatically. Sometimes, it was hard even to hold a conversation.

I would have to take a few shots of something strong to ease my nerves. After that investigation, I refused to take any medication that would lead to someone erroneously implying that I was illegally taking and hooked on drugs. I have a few of those in my family and that is one of the biggest insults a person could throw at me.

I didn't drink to get drunk nor did I like to drink in public, but I hated the fact that alcohol was the only way I could subsidize the tell signs that I was a stroke patient that had not fully recovered. To be honest, my pride kicked in overdrive, and I let that continue too long before deciding one day to ask for help.

It was never about being an addict. Actually, that was the part I hated about rehab. They forced you to admit to being an addict only to shove pills down your throat. It's worth noting that making people believe they need a prescribed drug to get over everything is just substituting one addiction for a more expensive one. That reminds me of someone going from marijuana to cocaine. You will keep chasing that first high or moment you felt the medicine worked best. I wasn't for that shit, and I made sure they knew it. I completed the program and came back to North Carolina.

Eventually, I realized that rehab wouldn't help me; only a lifestyle change could do that. I wasn't talking about some diet or exercise regimen. It was time to hang up my uniform for good. I was pushing through to prove something to people that no longer mattered. From that old NCOIC SFC Mitchell and his officer in charge (OIC) to CSM Ryder to my peers, these people were living their lives. I was living in the shadow of a career and lifestyle I might never get back.

I was gaining weight from the surgeries and the medicine that was prescribed and there was nothing I could do about it. I wasn't sloppy looking, but I wasn't the Sergeant Deligar that got himself promoted from E2 to E7 in nine years. I couldn't even lead my Soldiers in the best part of the day, physical fitness, anymore. I was tired of feeling defeated mentally and physically every day when I got home. My life had changed dramatically and I needed to find a new normal. Walking away from the military was actually one of the hardest decisions I have made. Not because of the pay, or false sense of power and authority, but because I really cared about every Soldier. I cared about their success. Furthermore, I cared about the Soldiers that they would eventually lead one day.

One day I sat with CSM Swygert, in his office, and expressed that I was done. That was the second hardest thing I had to do as a leader. CSM Swygert listened attentively and then encouraged me as only a man, fellow Soldier and senior leader could. When I walked into his office, I felt as though I was letting him down. When I left, I felt as though I had successfully done what he brought me there to do. The numbers didn't lie. Thank you, CSM Swygert, for not doing what I had seen so many leaders do time and time again. You didn't beat me down for choosing to take care of myself.

Within a few months, I had started my transition out of the Army. Some days, I miss it. Other days, I feel great about having the courage to walk away before it killed me. My last day of service to my country was February 26, 2019. Then 61 days later, my father died of a heart attack on his job. That shit broke my heart. I thought I had experienced heartbreak before, but I was WRONG!

There is no comparison to losing a parent, especially one that you admired and looked up to as much as I did my father. However, I felt that was a sign that time was worth more than money and pride at this point in my life.

My wife and daughter needed me more than what I could provide them. Fortunately, we have not missed a beat since I decided to leave the military. In fact, in October of that same year, after more than 14 years of failed attempts, Marketta and I found out we were having a baby. You don't know how much I really just needed to see God's hand in a miraculous way that year.

Iyana will always be my first child. But now I can know what it feels like to create something more valuable than money with the love of my life. Guys, I'm about to be a daddy again. I almost lost hope that it could even happen naturally. God did it. Well, technically, I "did it," but God made it happen.

Started to Lose Faith...

I was angry with God and started to question my belief system. Full transparency, I almost gave up on the notion that miracles could happen. Then, I remembered something that my childhood pastor used to always say, "God's timing, not ours." I even remembered the time I told my father I might not be able to have children of my own, and he simply said, "Twan, when its time, it will happen."

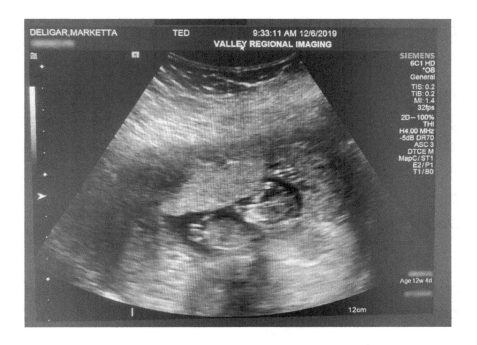

Well pops, this is one time I really wish you were here to see what I've done. But in a way, I kind of feel you saw this coming.

Hieu and Marquis,

You guys showed me that leadership should never be about telling people how good you are. Instead, you just do the work and let the results speak for themselves. Not only did you allow me to be a part of the team, but you made me feel like I deserved to be there.

You guys were the underrated pair. I truly believe my time under your command made me step out of my comfort zone and get my name and face out there.

This next section is just a few tips I learned through personal research and experience during my recovery.

As my auntie, Shon, would say, "Chew the meat and spit out the bones!"

What it felt like...

The TIA

Commonly referred to by medical personnel as a mini stroke.

- I felt dehydrated
- I had a really sharp pain behind my right eye. It actually felt like someone had stuck a needle through my eyeball.
- I lost peripheral vision in my left eye.
- It was misdiagnosed as a severe migraine due to my age.

The Ischemic Stroke

A stroke in which a blood clot blocks blood from passing through the blood vessel and reaching the brain. When I think of it, I think of that portion of the brain being starved and dying because of the lack of nutrients. Every subsequent image of my brain that has been taken, shows a dark spot where the stroke occurred. Strokes are a leading cause of death in the United States. If you believe you are having a stroke, call 9-1-1 immediately. It is worth noting, prompt treatment can help prevent brain damage and lasting effects.

- I felt nothing (no, seriously).
- I was telling my body to move, I was getting the sensation as though I was moving, but nothing was happening. I'm sure there is a medical term for it. The closest term I've found is phantom movement. It's commonly seen in amputee patients.
- My speech was slurring so much I sounded like a three-year-old trying to hold a conversation. I was thinking the words much faster than they were coming out. That freaked me out.

Pulmonary Embolism (PE)

Simply put, a blood clot is blocking a pulmonary artery in the lung.

- It started off feeling like a minor muscle spasm in my shoulder blade. For a couple of days, that spasm became more intense until, eventually, it turned into chest pain that stopped me in my tracks.
- I have never experienced a heart attack, but when we described my symptoms to the nurse on call, she advised us as if I were having one. She immediately told my wife to have me chew a baby aspirin and call 9-1-1.

Residual Effects (of my Stroke)

Stuttering and broken speech. There are times when I can speak fluidly and there are times when it is hard to get words to come out. My speech therapists believe that my speech is heavily driven by emotions. Most times, the higher my emotions/anxiety, the worst my speech gets.

Weakness on the right side of my body. I can still do most of the activities that I did before my stroke. But there are some things that I cannot.

I get tired more than usual. I like doing things that challenge my thought pattern, but I pay for it later. After retiring from the military, I chose to work in a field that requires me to do a lot of problem-solving because my neurologist recommended that I do puzzles and brain exercises daily to get back to normal as much as possible. The downside of that is that my speech becomes labored by the time I get home. I also tend to feel tired a lot. This might sound normal, but I didn't have this problem before my stroke.

Whenever I sit down to read or even during longer conversations, I find it hard to concentrate and comprehend things. It's a bit challenging because it requires me to read passages at a minimum of three times before retaining the information. I used to be quick on my feet. The fact that I notice a difference is a bit embarrassing at times. I get distracted very easily by noise and racing thoughts (which gets worse when I'm in a room that is too quiet).

I have to have soft music playing as a form of purposely distracting myself. I know that sounds crazy, but it works for me. It's also one of the reasons I have struggled with test-taking since my stroke. I have found that reading aloud is helping. I am currently pursuing my master's degree. Fortunately, the school has afforded me accommodations like longer time during tests and the ability to read aloud during proctored exams. If you are in this position, please don't let pride get in the way of rationale. Ask for help and accept it when it is offered.

More sensitive. Because I don't look like what I have been through or what I am going through, people tend to say and do some insensitive shit. Ranging from staring as you struggle to get words out to making comments about your weight. It is what it is. In my case, it's been "family and friends." I just chalk it up to their ignorance and tend to get a little ignorant back. You are different, accept it and keep it pushing. Don't let stupid people get you worked up. I typically just pray they never have to go through this experience.

Stress

Affects your mental health

When your body is under a lot of stress, sometimes you can find yourself depressed. What does depression look like? Well, it can present itself differently in many people. I am not a medical professional, so I will only speak to some of the signs that my family noticed. I was always separating myself. I did not find much pleasure in doing things. I never thought of it as depression because I was still highly functional, and depressed people sit in a corner and pity themselves, right? Wrong.

There are a lot of functional people that are depressed, and despite the stereotype, many do not want to commit suicide. They do not find pleasure in the company of others. It feels like work at times when they want to relax, which leads to anxiety.

Anxiety causes things like the racing of your heart, sweating of your hands, shaking, headaches, spinning rooms, and lightheadedness. In many veterans or trauma patients, it also causes us to experience discomfort in crowds or spaces where there are too many moving parts.

Affects your body

People dealing with stress may also experience some of the following issues in their body:

- Headaches
- Tense muscles or aches
- Insomnia
- Weakened Immune System

- Fertility issues
- Missed periods
- Low sex drive
- Erectile Dysfunction (ED)

Affects impulses

Stress can lead to an array of impulsive behaviors. Not only might you become more irritable, but you might also find yourself doing things that you probably would not have done at the rate you now seem to be doing them. Whether that be overeating, overspending, gambling, taking more risks, or even drinking heavily, you should be aware of these behaviors while under stress. Additionally, you want to be careful while taking prescription drugs and stay away from illegal narcotics.

The sense of relief that you may feel from those mood-altering drugs could become addictive. When you look at addiction as a result of stress, you must take into consideration the increased difficulty in recovery and staying sober. Please do not read what I am not saying. I am not saying that recovery or staying sober is impossible, but if you do not find a positive way to deal with that stress, your chances of relapse will increase.

Could lead to a stroke or heart attack

There is a part of the brain that deals with stress that is called the amygdala. Based on many tests performed, researchers believe that when there is a substantial amount of activity in this region of the brain, you are at a higher risk of stroke and heart disease. Again, if you are a minority reading this, please understand the risks are even higher for you. We have often been told that knowledge is power, but I think what many people miss is the implied task. It is easy to read and regurgitate information. However, when you gain an understanding through personal research and application, you are much more powerful and effective.

I want to leave you with a few notes: know what your stressors are, limit your stressors, and please do your annual checkups with your physician. There is a reason why they call stress the silent killer. After having my stroke, I had to change the way I retained information. Having worked in Information Technology for more than a decade, I have paralleled stress on the body to a mobile device running too many programs at the same time.

Without boring you too much, based on the hardware, specific devices can run several apps and programs at the same time without affecting the efficiency of the device. Others will start to slow down as your first warning. Next, you will probably notice specific functions not working correctly. Lastly, your phone will shut down to protect its mainframe. Sound familiar?

We make a lot of things in life more complicated than we need to because we place so much pressure on ourselves to be elevated by man. If you are a spiritual person, I challenge you to focus more on elevation by your higher power. If you are not religious, I challenge you to find your peace of mind and guard it.

How I Stay Motivated During the Storm...

Just as sure as you open your eyes every morning, you are guaranteed to face challenges. Some of those challenges could be the strength to get out of bed in the morning; dealing with rush hour traffic; dealing with that supervisor that is always riding you; dealing with those coworkers that you cannot stand, or maybe even just dealing with family that consistently uses and drains you of the little things you may have to give. Trust me; I have been there. I know the feeling, but I also know that you will never get anywhere worth going throwing a pity party for yourself over the things you cannot change.

I could easily use this platform to tell you everything will be alright and that you need to grow up. However, I know that it is not always that easy. I know that sometimes the very challenges we face daily quickly become our stressors. People are falling off the face of this earth daily because they let stressful situations bog them down and eventually kill them.

So how do I stay motivated when going through the storm? I stay humble. I realize that asking for help is not a weakness; it's an attribute of maturity and strength. Because I am a man of faith, I meditate and talk to my higher power. I also remind myself daily that the sun will rise, and all darkness must flee. I stay motivated through the storm by anticipating the delight I will feel when I eventually see the sun come out.

A little red-headed orphan once said that "the sun will come out tomorrow." Christopher Robbin's best friend, Winnie the Pooh, once said, "I always get to where I'm going by walking away from where I've been." So how do I stay motivated through the storm? I stay focused on where I want to be and not where I am when the storm comes.

Listen, nobody can tell you how to deal with your storm. Nobody can adequately prepare you for the storm you might face. But what can be provided to you are tools to help you keep your sanity, maintain your faith, and overcome.

Here are a few suggested tips:

Tips 1: Find something that makes you happy and do it daily. I'm still working on that.

Tip 2: Learn to meditate. Meditation does not have to be religious if that's not your thing. Meditation is merely finding a place of peace inside you. Find a place where, no matter how loud the noise around you may get, you can go there and find comfort and rest.

Tip 3: Surround yourself with people who speak positive and affirm you. Negative people are like a plague waiting to devour anything that has life.

Tip 4: Try substituting wasted time with positive habits like reading or listening to audiobooks and podcasts. I am an avid music lover and television watcher. I have learned to step away from both for a while during the day and listen to audiobooks that talk about ways to be successful and build wealth. I have also gained a lot of insight into my private life by listening to many of those books or podcasts.

Tip 5: Focus on your lane. Think of it as driving an automobile. When you get on the main road, you cannot worry about what the person next to you is doing in their car. Doing so would eventually cause you to miss a hazard and become one yourself.

Tip 6: Do not compare your life to anyone else's. If we believed everything people post on social media, we would be led to believe that everyone is happy and living their best life. Or to think that no one is facing financial hardships, trouble at work, trouble at school, abuse, or divorce. As much as I would like that to be true, people lie to appear normal. But you cannot focus that. You should not even focus on revealing the lie. Instead, focus on your journey and live your truth.

Applying these tips will not always bring immediate relief, but they will remind you that beyond wishing and praying for better days you can do your part to make the life you live a better one.

Iyana and Lorraine,

You guys have been by my side through some pretty tough moments. The moves I have made in the last four years have been with you both in mind. Iyana, you are and have always been my reason to fight. There a lot of things you didn't understand growing up, and I know it may have appeared as though you were second to my job. Nothing could be further from the truth. My sacrifice then was for the moments we share now. However, I wish I knew more balance back then.

Raine, since the moment I knew you existed, your G-momma and I didn't hesitate to interject ourselves into your life. You are a blessed young lady to have the type of love that surrounds you daily. But we are all better people to have such a light in our lives.

I love you both and hope to be a better example of at least the minimum a man must be to win you over. MUCH LATER IN LIFE, OF COURSE!

Letter to my baby sister

Miah,

It is for you that I pushed and pressed on. Still a young boy myself, as your big brother, pop always told me that I was responsible for you whether I liked it or not. He said that you would look at the good and bad things I do, and those behaviors would become your examples in life. I took a lot of spankings, but pop always knew that our relationship was closer than any relationship we could have with him or mom. He wanted us to embrace that bond because he knew one day it would just be you and I.

I believe he was counting on us to cherish and protect our bond from any and everyone. So that is what we will continue to do. I know I am not your father, but I am the rightful successor to the throne of Hezekiah Deligar III. You are an heiress to that kingdom. As a part of his legacy, you are his greatest investment. You are the valuable stock that pays dividends. I got you!

About the author

Antwan Deligar was born and raised in Jacksonville, Fl. He is the older of two children. He left Jacksonville to join the military in 2007. Since then, Antwan, his wife, Marketta and their daughter, Iyana, have embarked on a journey like no other learning each other and themselves. A first-time author, Antwan hopes to reach you or someone you know through his transparency. He is passionate about helping others and hopes that his message does not get lost in translation. In terms of health (no matter the category), you must take care of yourself because there will never be another you.

For booking information please email adeligar@imagconglomerate.com.